OXFORD

The ancient and historic buildings of Oxford University cover an area of less than half a square mile, roughly within the limits of the old City wall—the original colleges, with their chapels, halls and libraries, the places in which those who have come to enjoy this rich heritage, live and work. The story of Oxford reflects in a unique way the history of England in all its aspects; in these pages an effort has been made to let these buildings, in their incomparable settings, tell that story for themselves, through photographs which show without adornment, the architectural splendour which has made Oxford a place of pilgrimage for the world.

THEIR AMBITION TO PRODUCE THIS VERY BEST BOOK ON OXFORD
David and Emmeline 'Bill' Thomas partners in the production of the first edition of 'Oxford the Golden Heart of Britain' working at 'roof level' with large format 'Sinar' camera and wide choice of lens to produce the pictures in this book.

ISBN 0–9501337–0–1

Illustrated by J. W. Thomas, MA Oxon, ARPS

© Published by Thomas-Photos, Oxford.
1 Collinwood Close, Headington, Oxford.

Printed in Great Britain by
S & S Press, Abingdon

THE SPIRES

It was Matthew Arnold who wrote the immortal lines—"And that sweet City with the dreaming spires. She needs not June for beauty's heightening". A glimpse of a corner of the famous Oxford skyline.

FOREWORD

By SIR WILLIAM HAYTER, KCMG

Warden of New College, Oxford, 1958–76

'On an eminence of scarcely perceptible elevation, at the confluence of the rivers Isis and Cherwell, in the bosom of a delightful valley, surrounded by luxuriant meadows, and, at greater distance, environed by gently swelling hills, which smile in all the pride of cultivated beauty, and are richly diversified by hanging woods, stands the fair City . . '

THESE opening words of Wade's eighteenth-century 'Walks in Oxford' inspire some nostalgia in a modern reader. The 'delightful valley' and the 'luxuriant meadows', even the 'gently swelling hills', are now mostly built over and industrialised. But inside this outer ring of development there still lies, almost untouched, the little old inner city, the golden heart of Oxford. Its streets are often noisy and crowded, but it is possible to step off them, through porter's lodges or dark gateways, into the total peace and quiet of a garden or a quadrangle. And these streets, gardens and quadrangles are surrounded, dominated and embellished by buildings of extraordinary variety and charm. No town in England, and perhaps no town anywhere, contains within so small a space so much good architecture, covering so wide a period of history.

Oxford owes almost all these buildings to the University and its Colleges. There are of course a few buildings that were here before the University came into existence in the thirteenth century. The Romans built nothing in Oxford, perhaps did not even settle here. But when architecture began again in England after the Dark Ages it began here too. The oldest monument in Oxford, someone once said, is not a building at all but Port Meadow, the great open space of land along the Isis, north of Oxford, that has belonged since our history began to the Freemen of Oxford. Our oldest surviving building is the Saxon tower of St. Michael's in the Cornmarket, and there is early Norman work in the Castle tower and at St. Peter's in the East. Of the great monastic buildings of the pre-University period the only remains are the Norman work in what is now the Cathedral. But once the University and the Colleges had established themselves, almost all the interesting buildings in Oxford were put up by them; the handsome eighteenth-century City Church of All Saints' was the only important exception, and even that has now become the library of Lincoln College.

The foreigner who visits Oxford sometimes asks 'But where is the University?' It is not an easy question to answer. Our visitor is thinking of the universities in his home country, compact, square, self-contained buildings easily identifiable for what they are. In this sense there is no 'University' in Oxford. The nearest we have to it is the fine series of buildings that reaches from the eastern end of Broad Street, down Catte Street, to the High Street. This is indeed the heart of the heart of Oxford, containing some of Oxford's noblest buildings, of varying dates and yet all living harmoniously together. The University Church of St. Mary the Virgin on the High Street has the best of all Oxford's spires, and a magnificent seventeenth-century porch, one of the most exuberant bits of baroque in England. Then comes the Radcliffe Camera, now the main reading room of the University library, built by Gibbs in the more restrained baroque of the eighteenth-century. England as a country lacks fine domes; after St. Paul's the Camera is perhaps the grandest we possess. Then we come to what is the nearest to being 'the University' in the continental sense, the Old Schools Quadrangle, now the Bodleian Library, four-square and plain outside but with a highly decorated courtyard and containing some beautiful rooms, the best being perhaps the fifteenth-century Divinity School with its elaborate vaulting. North of this again is the Clarendon Building, originally the University Press and now a Bodleian Library Annexe, designed by Hawksmoore in his grandest and most formidable manner. Next to it is the Sheldonian Theatre, one of Wren's earliest works, which provides a lavish setting for University ceremonial, and beyond it the Old Ashmolean, the oldest museum building in the world.

Thus if we cannot point to a single building as 'the University', we have in the centre of Oxford a group of buildings, containing most of the central functions of the University, of a grandeur with which few other universities can compete. It must be said that the buildings put up by the University subsequently are not in this class. It is best not to dwell on the New Bodleian across Broad Street. The Science Area, to the north, is a grave of architectural reputations. The new Ashmolean Museum, handsome in its Greek Revival way, is on a cramped site which inhibits the proper display of its remarkable treasures. The new University Offices in Wellington Square are dull and insignificant.

HERTFORD COLLEGE

Oxford's 'Bridge of Sighs', built to provide a graceful link between the old and new buildings of Hertford College, seen against the incomparable background of the bell tower of New College in its sylvan setting. The new buildings incorporate the former Chapel of Our Lady at Smithgate—an unusual octagonal structure dating from the sixteenth century which occupies the site of one of the bastions in the old City Wall.

The University has redeemed these later failures by providing the city with some fine open spaces. The University Parks, with their specimen trees and their romantic riverside walk, seem now to be safe from the encroaching scientists. And the Botanic Garden, with its classical layout, walls, urns and fountains, its views of college towers, its glimpses of the river, added to all its horticultural attractions, is one of the most delightful places in Oxford.

So the University has on the whole done its best to embellish the city in which it finds itself. But it must be said that the greatest contribution to Oxford's architectural heritage has been made, over the centuries, by the Colleges. To grasp the extent of this we must try to visualise the plan of the old city. This is quite simple. It is more or less square, and divided into four quarters by two main arteries, the High Street (prolonged by Queen Street) running east and west, and the north-south line of St. Aldates and the Cornmarket. These two lines cross at Carfax. The two eastern quarters of the city, except in the immediate neighbourhood of Carfax, are almost entirely occupied by the Colleges, with the University enclave, already described, north of the High Street. There are a few Colleges to the north and west, but the main concentration is in the great cluster in the eastern half, on both sides of the High Street, between Carfax and the Cherwell.

The High Street itself is one of the most beautiful streets in the world. Wordsworth wrote of 'the stream-like winding of that glorious street', and it is still true that, as you walk up it, its successive curves bring each moment a new and splendid building into view. It is lined, at its eastern end, with Colleges interspersed with smaller buildings, and down the lanes and alleys leading off it are grouped most of the rest.

This eastern half of the old city shows a really extraordinary concentration of ancient buildings, almost unparalleled elsewhere. Every College has its own chapel, dining-hall, and library grouped with other buildings round two or more quadrangles. There are more or less grand lodgings for the Head of the College, rooms for Fellows and undergraduates, common-rooms, kitchens, beer-cellars. Many of the Colleges have large gardens. Some have cloisters. Their buildings date from the thirteenth to the twentieth centuries, but the great majority of them were built between the years 1400 and 1800. Except in Cambridge, there is nothing else like them.

The two oldest foundations, University College and Balliol, have nothing architectural to attest their antiquity. The present buildings of University College are almost all of the seventeenth-century; its most interesting feature is the glowing Flemish glass in the chapel. Balliol, so distinguished academically, is an architectural desert, though its tree-dotted layout is agreeable and conducive to social life.

The architectural history of the Oxford Colleges really begins with the third foundation, Merton, with its fine thirteenth-century chapel, like the church of a good-sized Cotswold priory, its library, perhaps the oldest in the world, and Mob Quad, the first of the Oxford quadrangles. The three next foundations in date, Exeter, Oriel and Queen's, again have nothing of their original antiquity to show. Exeter's chief distinction is one of the most consistent creations of the Gothic Revival in Oxford, its chapel as rebuilt by Gilbert Scott in imitation of the Sainte Chapelle. Oriel has an agreeable seventeenth-century quadrangle and a fine, plain eighteenth-century library by James Wyatt. Queen's, though founded in 1340, is now entirely of the eighteenth-century, with a splendid baroque front to the High Street and a chapel, dining-hall and very grand library in the same imposing style.

New College, founded in 1379, was the first complete college to be built, all in one go and all to one plan, with all the appurtenances that colleges have since been thought to need. Its chapel, hall, library, front quadrangle, cloisters and bell-tower were all built between 1379 and 1402 and are all, except the library, still in use for the purpose for which they were built. It has been much altered since, not always to advantage, and its buildings tend to have a somewhat austere look, particularly from without. But there are great treasures inside (above all in the chapel, the largest and in many ways the finest in Oxford), while the cloisters and the garden, which is backed by the only remaining complete sector of the City Wall, are delightful.

Two colleges which were originally closely modelled on New College are Magdalen and All Souls. Magdalen has combined its cloister with its main quadrangle into a complete unit, dominated by its magnificent bell-tower, the most beautiful in Oxford, that greets the traveller from London as he enters the old city. Behind the original fifteenth-century building lie a grand eighteenth-century block, a deer park with a herd of fallow-deer, and Addison's Walk, a charming triangle of paths among trees along the Cherwell, where rare fritillaries grow in the spring. All Souls, originally smaller than the other two, enlarged itself in the eighteenth-century with a twin-towered Gothick fantasy designed by Hawksmoor.

THE TURL

Dominating the High Street entrance to the Turl is the library of Lincoln College, formerly the City Church. The Turl, which connects 'the Broad' with 'the High', contains three colleges—Exeter, Lincoln and Jesus. It gets its unusual name from a 'twirl' or turnstile which was placed in a narrow postern in the old city wall at the north end . . . "to keepe horses and the other cattle out of the city when a faire was kept in Canditch".

Then there are the three Colleges along Turl Street. Exeter has already been mentioned. The buildings of Jesus were mainly put up in the late sixteenth and early seventeenth-century. So were those of Lincoln, although the College was actually founded in 1427. Lincoln backs onto Brasenose, which at its other end presents an agreeable seventeenth-century front to Radcliffe Square and All Souls. This group of Colleges contains many pleasing features of the early seventeenth-century, a period when Gothic architecture, long extinct elsewhere, lingered on nostalgically in Oxford, often tricked out with a certain amount of Renaissance detail. Corpus Christi College, on the other side of the High Street, also belongs to this class, and is further embellished by a very handsome Fellows Building of the eighteenth-century.

However, the great foundation of this period is unquestionably Christ Church, the largest and grandest of all the Oxford Colleges. Tom Quadrangle, itself larger than any other in Oxford, was started by Cardinal Wolsey. Impressive as it is, it was meant to be even more so, with cloister walks on all four sides and, on the north, a chapel to rival King's College Chapel at Cambridge. All this was interrupted by Wolsey's fall, and when Henry VIII completed the foundation he discarded the plans for the Cardinal's chapel and decided to retain what was left of St. Frideswide's Abbey church (which Wolsey had begun to demolish), adapting it for use not only as a chapel for Christ Church but as the cathedral of the new diocese of Oxford. Christ Church cathedral is not among the more imposing of English cathedrals, but it has many charms; its spire is said to be the oldest in the country. And the loss of Wolsey's buildings in Tom Quadrangle is to some degree compensated for by the building of Wren's superb Tom Tower over the main gate, and by the grand eighteenth-century buildings, the library and Peckwater Quadrangle, to the north. On the other side of the House Christ Church Meadow provides Oxford with one of its most attractive open spaces and leads down to the Thames with its barges and boat-houses.

At about the same time Colleges began to appear on the far side of the old city of Oxford, outside the north wall which ran (and in part, hidden behind houses, still runs) just south of the present line of Broad Street. These were Trinity, founded in 1554, of which the principal feature is an elegant, and elegantly furnished, eighteenth-century chapel, St. John's, founded the next year, with a beautiful arcaded Laudian quadrangle, and Wadham, founded in 1612, perhaps the last major Gothic (as opposed to revived Gothic) building in the world. All these Colleges, being outside the city walls, have extensive and beautiful gardens.

Only two of the ancient foundations are west of the St. Aldates-Cornmarket line. These are Pembroke, Dr. Johnson's College, and Worcester, with one of Oxford's largest gardens and buildings which are partly mediaeval cells for members of now dissolved Benedictine monasteries studying in Oxford and partly in the grand classical manner of the late eighteenth-century.

Besides the Colleges in the old city there used to be numerous smaller institutions called Halls. Most of these were swallowed up by the Colleges (the physical remains of one of them, St. Mary's Hall, can be seen within Oriel). Only one retains an independent existence. This is St. Edmund Hall, which traces its history back to the thirteenth-century but which did not become a full College until 1956. Its little quadrangle, with all the features of a College in miniature, is one of the most attractive in Oxford. Hertford College occupies the site of several Halls that have since disappeared. Its most notable feature is the bridge spanning New College Lane. This was built in the early years of this century to connect the older quadrangle with a newer one across the lane, and is now more photographed by tourists than any of the more ancient monuments of Oxford.

The newer Colleges, foundations of the nineteenth and twentieth-centuries, are scattered round the perimeter of the old city, mostly to the north and west. Few of them are of great architectural interest. Keble, built all in one by Butterfield, and St. Catherine's, built all in one by Arne Jacobsen, are the most notable contributions of the last and the present centuries respectively; both already attract admiring visitors.

This brief scurry round the beauties of Oxford has inevitably omitted many of them. Wade had more time and more space in his leisurely eighteenth-century 'Walks'. On the other hand, he lacked the advantage of Mr. Thomas's splendid photographs.

THE SHELDONIAN THEATRE

The Sheldonian Theatre, given to the University by Gilbert Sheldon, Archbishop of Canterbury and Chancellor of the University, was designed by Christopher Wren when he was Savilian Professor of Astronomy at Oxford. It was inaugurated "with the greatest *splendor* and formalitie" on July 9, 1669. It was the first large-scale work of the architect, who based his original plans for the new building on the Theatre of Marcellus in Rome, a scheme which proved far too extravagant in view of the money available, and new plans were produced. The purpose of the building was to provide a suitable setting for university ceremonies and in particular "The Act"—the forerunner of the present-day Encaenia (thanksgiving)—which took place in St. Mary's Church and had in recent years become something of a scandal for a sacred edifice. It was also to house the University Printer, but eventually his business encroached into the area of the Theatre itself and other arrangements had to be made. The result of storing heavy loads of books in the attics was a deterioration in the roof timbers, an ingenious and complicated structure, without cross-beams and supported only by braces and screws, which had to be replaced at the beginning of the nineteenth century. The splendid ceiling, 70 feet by 80 feet, was painted by Robert Streeter, Sergeant Painter to the Crown in sections which were brought to Oxford from London by water. It was designed to suggest a Roman theatre, open to the sky, with gilded ropes stretching from side to side supporting a red drapery which could be unfurled by cherubs to protect the audience. Each panel is a self-contained composition, and the subject is allegorical, symbolising the Restoration with Religion and the Arts triumphing over Envy, Malice, Rapine and Ignorance. The Sheldonian was completely restored inside and out by the Oxford Historic Buildings Fund and is seen at its best at the Encaenia in June, after the end of the summer term, when the University honours distinguished men and women from all parts of the world.

WADHAM COLLEGE

Like so many other Oxford colleges, Wadham occupies the site of a much older religious foundation, the former home of the Austin Friars, which had fallen into disuse after the Dissolution and been bought by the city authorities, who were later made to sell it for its new purpose. It is a monument to a devoted couple, Nicholas Wadham, a Somerset gentleman, and his wife Dorothy. Nicholas died in 1609, before his dream of founding a college in Oxford for members of the Church of England—he was discussing plans for his scheme only a few days before his death—were realised, but his widow carried out his wishes. Letters Patent for the new society were granted by the King in 1613 and in April of that year the first members were admitted to the university. Most of them came from the west country—Somerset, Devon and Dorset, as did the craftsmen who erected the buildings and the connection is still maintained. It is a lovely place, the main entrance approached between trim lawns, and the front quadrangle, a perfect specimen, still as its builders left it, save that the lawn round which the buildings are grouped, was only laid down at the beginning of the last century. On three sides are the rooms which house its members, and on the fourth are chapel and hall, over the entrance to which stand statues of the founders, surmounted by that of the first Stuart monarch. Both chapel and hall are noted for their rich woodwork, embellished by carvers who were artists as well as craftsmen. The hall has a glorious hammer-beam roof and an elaborate screen, while the chapel is 'a veritable treasure house of fine woodcarving', with its box pews, and choir stalls, pulpit and panelling and not least the elegant screen. The altar table is Jacobean and was brought from Ilminster, where the Founders are buried, less than a hundred years ago. The windows contain some of the finest seventeenth century glass in Oxford, and that in the east window is the work of the famous Dutchman, Bernard Van Linge, depicting scenes from the last days in Jerusalem, for which, as the accounts show, he was paid £113 17s. 5d. Sir Christopher Wren is among the most famous Wadham men, and according to tradition designed the clock above the ante-chapel, the original mechanism of which is still preserved in the Museum of the History of Science. Considerable building has taken place since the last war, chiefly to provide for an increased number of undergraduates.

ST. EDMUND HALL

The miniature quadrangle of St. Edmund Hall in the shadow of the massive bulk of Queen's College and what was one of the city's oldest and finest churches until it was converted into a Library for the Hall, is one of the most charming corners of Oxford.

It occupies a unique position as the last of the medieval halls and can claim to be the oldest academical society for the education of undergraduates still surviving in the University. Tradition has long associated it as the site of the house where Edmund of Abingdon, the first Oxford scholar to become Archbishop of Canterbury and the first to be canonized, lived while he taught at the University. At what date the future Saint's house was converted into a hall is not known, but about 1270 the property was given to Osney Abbey which rented it to a succession of tenants throughout the medieval period. Grouped round the front quadrangle which, as has been said "preserved the very quintessence of the charm of Oxford", are buildings which represent every century, from the Middle Ages to the present time. Since 1937, the Hall has enjoyed full collegiate status, and since the last war, has made such progress that large-scale development became necessary. One of the most picturesque features of the main quadrangle is the well in the centre which provided the Hall's first water supply. It was re-opened in 1927 and a new well-head built over it. Down to the sixteenth century the water was drawn by windlass and bucket, but later lead pipes were inserted and the water drawn by two pumps. The Canterbury Building was completed in 1934 to commemorate the 700th anniversary of the consecration of St. Edmund as Archbishop.

THE RADCLIFFE CAMERA

Oxford has two centres—Carfax where the city's four main roads meet in a swirl of traffic and a little to the east, the Radcliffe Camera looming in tranquil majesty in its noble setting. It provides a magnificent memorial to one of Oxford's greatest sons, Dr. John Radcliffe, graduate of University College, Fellow of Lincoln College and a famous and fashionable physician. He was noted for being outspoken, and he did not hesitate to treat his Royal patients with the same candour as ordinary folk. He offended both Queen Anne and her brother-in-law William the Third, the former Prince of Orange, particularly when he told the dropsical monarch that he would not have his "two legs for his two kingdoms". But he amassed a fortune, most of which was devoted to good causes and particularly to his old university. He died in 1714. His executors were instructed to pay £40,000 to the University over a ten-year period for the purpose of building a new library "between St. Maries and the scholes in Catstreet". The site was occupied by a number of tenement houses belonging to different owners and because of this, there were complications, with the result that negotiations dragged on for more than twenty years, and it was not until 1737 that the foundation stone of the new building was laid. Several architects were considered. James Gibbs was chosen and his brilliant design is the earliest example of a circular library in England. It has two storeys with a particularly fine staircase. Completed in 1748, it was not opened until the following year when it was intended to accommodate "All Sorts of books, belonging to the Science of Physic and Anatomy, Botany, Surgery and Philosophy", but it was not until 1811 that its contents were confined to scientific works.

The basement was originally an open arcade with a vaulted stone ceiling, the aisles of which were covered by iron grilles, three of which formed gates to give access to the library. At one time it housed the university fire engine and in the French scare of 1859 the University Rifle Volunteers drilled there. In 1863 the arches were glazed, the new outside staircase was built and the space made available became a reading room. The building is now used as a reading room and in 1927 it was made over to the University by the Radcliffe Trustees.

THE DIVINITY SCHOOL

Underneath Duke Humfrey's library is the Divinity School, built also in the fifteenth century. Work started on it in 1423, but went on fitfully, partly owing to lack of money and partly because Henry VI attracted away the craftsmen engaged on it, to work on his buildings at Eton and St. George's Chapel, Windsor. It was not finished until 1483. It is one of Oxford's most noble buildings, with its walls nearly all windows from which the stained glass disappeared at the Reformation. But the splendour of the medieval roof remains, with its fan-vaulting, painted bosses and the delicately carved pendants, each of which contains a tiny figure.

THE RADCLIFFE CAMERA   The full splendour of the building is best seen from the tower of the University Church.

ALL SOULS COLLEGE

What more magnificent war memorial could be envisaged than a college, such as 'the college of All Souls of the Faithful Departed in Oxford' which was founded to commemorate those who died, on both sides, in the French wars. It was built and endowed by Henry Chichele, Archbishop of Canterbury, to educate and increase the number of secular clergy . . . "a college of poor and indigent clerks, bound with all devotion to pray for the Souls of the glorious memory of Henry V, lately King of England and France, the Duke of Clarence and the other Lords and Lieges of the realm of England, whom the havoc of that warfare, between the two realms . . ." The foundation Charter was granted on May 20, 1438, by Henry VI, son of the victor of Agincourt who, became co-founder. The site was in the heart of the University, on one side of the narrow Catte Street, opposite the University Church of St. Mary and building began immediately. The accounts are still preserved, and record the cost down to the last farthing. The first buildings were along the High Street, and they were ready for use in 1442, while the first Mass was celebrated in the chapel in the same year, less than twelve months before the Archbishop's death. Much of the original buildings remain, though altered and changed, but they might have disappeared altogether had plans for a wholesale rebuilding been carried out in the eighteenth century. It was largely due to the persistence of Hawksmoor, the architect, who opposed the plan, that with the exception of the fifteenth century hall and cloisters, they were preserved. He is commemorated by the splendid second quadrangle to the north of the original building, dominated by the lovely twin towers, and completed by the cloisters and the handsome gate giving on to Radcliffe Square. One of the most notable rooms is the old library, now used as a lecture room, with its handsome plaster ceiling and fire-place, which dates from the time of the first Elizabeth. The chapel is the only one in Oxford to be without an organ. With so many of its other adornments, the pair of organs which had been given by the Founder were destroyed at the Reformation. The medieval glass survived, only to disappear later, it is thought, during the time when Oxford was occupied by the Parliament troops at the end of the Civil War. The Codrington Library was the gift of Colonel Christopher Codrington, a soldier who fought in Flanders with William III, and later a colonial Governor, a former Fellow of the college who bequeathed £6,000 and his collection of books. The foundation stone was laid in June 1716 but the work dragged on for over thirty years and it was not until 1751 that it was finally completed. Apart from the original collection of books it contains many treasures, among them the collection of Sir Christopher Wren's drawings for the rebuilding of London after the great fire. Another famous feature of the quadrangle is the elaborate sundial erected in 1658-9. Wren was Bursar at the time and because the ingenious dial records the minutes as well as the hours of the day, it is considered that he designed the handsome addition to the college amenities. The college has no undergraduates, only Doctors and Masters, as its members. It used to have what were known as 'Bible Clerks' a little community of four undergraduates, who on weekdays read the lessons in chapel, and were taught and accommodated, but this unique survival of the past is no more.

ALL SOULS COLLEGE   The outstanding feature of the college is provided by the lovely twin towers, glimpsed through a gateway in Radcliffe Square.

NEW COLLEGE

When William of Wykeham, born in the tradition common for high-ranking ecclesiastics of his time, of poor and humble parents, founded his 'St. Mary College of Winchester in Oxford'—commonly called New College, he chose for its site what must surely have been the most unsavoury of any available. He acquired a piece of vacant land in the north-east angle of the city walls, a space "littered with dead dogs, cats and other rubbish", scarred with gravel and sand pits which was the haunt of robbers and murderers. The owners were only too glad to sell the land, one access to which was through a postern gate in the walls into 'Hell Passage', appropriately named in view of the reputation of the place. In due course, a Royal Licence to found the college was granted but one condition was imposed—the City wall had to be kept in repair and access permitted to the City authorities for the purposes of inspection and, of course, for defence if ever that need should arise. In addition, two posterns, one at each end of the property were to be made so that the Mayor and his colleagues might make an entrance every three years to see that the conditions were being fulfilled. This ancient custom is still continued. It was revived in 1957, a year when the college made extensive repairs to the walls, by the late Warden Smith, after a lapse of many years. The Lord Mayor and such members of the Corporation as choose to accompany him, enter by the special doorway in Queen's Lane, perambulate the walls accompanied by the Warden and Fellows, after which they are entertained to suitable refreshment. Oxford was an easy place to defend, with the river on three sides, but some artificial defences had existed since very early times. The walls, as they exist now, were rebuilt in the reign of King Henry III. In 1327 the Mayor and Burgesses were allowed to levy toll on all carts bringing produce for sale into the City. Repairs were carried out in 1370 and 1371 towards the cost of which a general tax was levied on everyone, the religious having to pay as well as the ordinary folk. The best view of the walls is obtained from the college gardens and it gives an excellent idea of how a fortified town was defended in medieval times. Massive bastions were built at frequent intervals, the object of which was to ensure that every yard of ground outside could be kept under observation by the defenders, who could cover it and any attackers with raking fire without exposing themselves to the enemy. A walk wide enough to allow the defenders to pass each other as they moved from one bastion to another to take up position, runs along the top of the wall, which is protected by breast high battlements. In fact, these imposing defences were never used; no archers loosed their arrows through the slits inserted into the masonry for this purpose, nor was molten lead or boiling pitch poured from the top on to anyone unlucky enough to be sheltering at the bottom. It would seem that the college buildings themselves had been planned with defence in mind. Chapel and hall, built—unusually—end to end, with their great stained glass windows, are placed on the north side where they were protected by the city walls and ditch; the bell tower, the most lofty feature of the college, replaces one of the bastions. New College is the first example in Oxford of a college planned to include all the buildings necessary for the life of a society; chapel and hall, bell tower, warden's lodgings, library and kitchen and other domestic offices are grouped together.

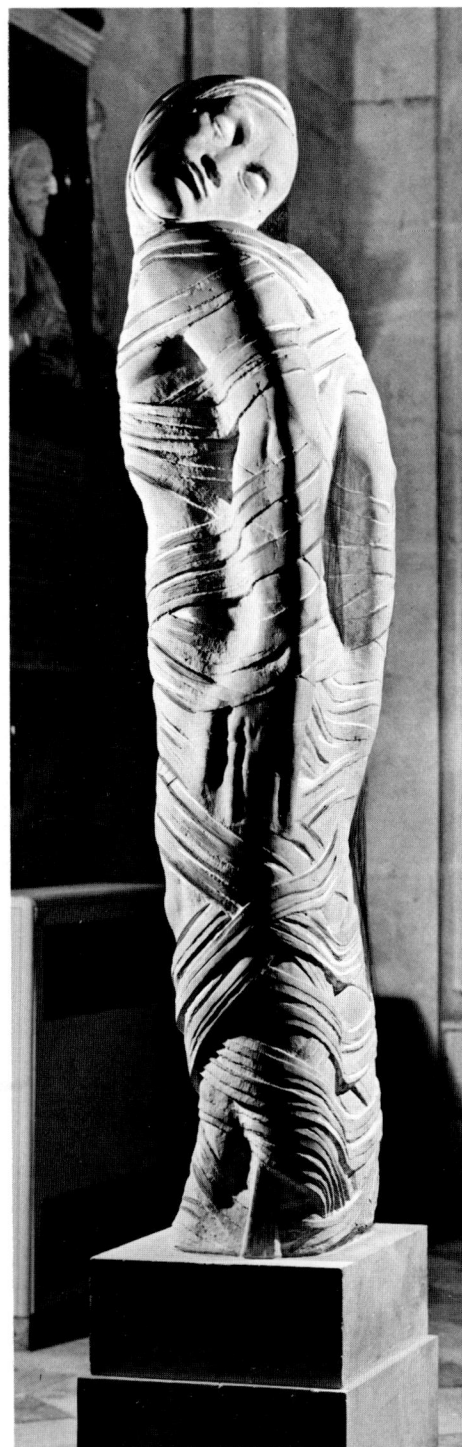

EPSTEIN'S LAZARUS

NEW COLLEGE   Visitors who go through the narrow entrance to the college find themselves in a
large quadrangle, dominated on the north side by the chapel.

The main entrance in a narrow lane, hemmed in by high grey walls, with a bridge built slightly askew over a bend in the lane, gives no hint of the glories which lie behind this forbidding approach. The foundation stone was laid in 1380, the first members were in occupation seven years later and the whole was completed, with cloisters and bell-tower, by 1400. Later another storey was added to the front quadrangle, spoiling its proportions, and in 1682 the charming garden quadrangle was built, with a handsome iron gateway through which a vista of one of the loveliest gardens in Oxford opens out, against the background of the ancient walls. The mound in the centre is artificial. It was begun in 1529 and has undergone numerous changes and embellishments since.

New College chapel is one of the finest in Oxford, and its original plan has provided the model for others built later. Throughout the centuries it has been continuously altered and restored so that only the shell remains as it was when the builders had completed their work. The eastern wall, which is also the western wall of the magnificent hall, was completely covered by a reredos, the niches and carvings of which were coloured in blue and gold. This lovely work was completely destroyed at the Reformation but in the nineteenth century, during restoration work, some fragments were found. The present reredos is a reconstruction of the original from these pieces and the niches are filled with statues of angels, archangels, apostles, saints, martyrs and prophets. Most of the ancient stained glass in the Ante-Chapel survived the destruction wrought by the reformers, because the college claimed it was too poor to provide replacements for the windows which would have been destroyed. On one side of the altar is displayed one of the college's most prized possessions—the Founder's pastoral staff which, with other personal relics he bequeathed to its members in his will, made in 1403, the year before his death at the age of 80. It is a magnificent specimen of medieval craftsmanship, 6 ft. 9 in. long and in two parts—the shaft, and the crook which surmounts an elaborate capital. Made of iron, overlaid with silver gilt, it provides a perfect example of very elaborate tabernacle work. Dominating the west end of the chapel, underneath the unusual window designed by Sir Joshua Reynolds, is Epstein's statue of Lazarus, bought by the college nearly twenty years ago. Nearly 8 ft. high and weighing a ton and a half, it depicts Lazarus, his arms bound with burial bandages, standing on the threshold of life and death, looking over his shoulder as he is resurrected. The Reynolds window shows in the upper part the Nativity and the Adoration of the Shepherds, with representations of the seven Virtues beneath.

NEW COLLEGE
The reredos, which occupies the eastern wall, is a tribute to 19th century craftsmen who built it to a design revealed by fragments discovered during restoration. The original was destroyed at the Reformation.

THE FOUNDER'S CROZIER

THE BODLEIAN LIBRARY

The Schools Quadrangle, dominated by the famous Tower of Five Orders, has been wholly part of the Bodleian Library since 1884, but its buildings go back for centuries before that. There is the incomparable Divinity School which was begun at the beginning of the fifteenth century, and then Duke Humfrey's Library, named after the Duke of Gloucester, brother of Henry V, who was wounded at Agincourt, through whose munificence it was built and equipped a few years later. The remainder of the quadrangle was built by the University between 1613 and 1618 to provide rooms for lectures and academic exercises, the subjects of which are still painted over the doors on the ground floor. Sir Thomas Bodley, scholar and Elizabethan diploma-tist, who was responsible for re-founding Duke Humfrey which had been allowed to fall into decay from the time of Edward VI onwards, added a third storey to provide more room for books which poured in from benefactors including himself. In 1789 the Bodleian took over the old School of Medicine for library purposes and in the years that followed, gradually absorbed the rest of the schools. The lofty tower illustrates the five orders of architecture—Tuscan, Doric, Ionic, Corinthian and Composite, and adorning the facade of the fourth storey is a stone figure of King James I underneath a canopy, presenting copies of his works to Fame, who is on his right hand and the University on his left. The bronze statue standing at the entrance to the library and Divinity School is of William Herbert, Earl of Pembroke, Chancellor of the University at the time. The massive door leading into Catte Street is contemporary with the building and on it are displayed the coats of arms of the seventeen colleges which existed in 1619. It is opened only on special ceremonial occasions.

THE SCHOOLS QUADRANGLE

DUKE HUMFREY'S LIBRARY

The glorious painted ceiling of Duke Humfrey library, built in the fifteenth century to hou the collection of books given by the Duke Gloucester, brother of Henry V.

CORPUS CHRISTI COLLEGE

Sandwiched between an older and a younger neighbour—Merton and Christ Church—Corpus Christi College was founded in 1516 by Richard Foxe, the holder of four bishoprics in turn, and was the last to be established in Oxford before the Reformation.

His service to Henry VII earned the future Bishop the royal favour which extended throughout the reign of his son, Henry VIII, whom he had baptised. He had also been Master of Pembroke College, Cambridge and Chancellor of that University, but it was on Oxford that he showered the wealth he accumulated, and the college with which he enriched it is a noble memorial to a great and generous man. The main quadrangle, with the hall and chapel, remain as they were built in his time, but its dominant feature, a tall sundial, came later. It was raised by a Fellow of the college, Charles Turnbull in 1581 and is of curious design, with a perpetual calendar on the pillar, a square block carved with the coats of arms of the founder, his friend Hugh Oldham, Bishop of Exeter and a generous benefactor, the Queen and Oxford. Surmounting it is a pelican, the bird chosen by Foxe to be the emblem of his college. The chapel was extensively restored in 1675, and its chief treasure is the altar piece, a Rubens painting of the Adoration of the Shepherds. The college also still possesses the pastoral staff of the founder, a magnificent piece of medieval craftsmanship, and a finer collection of plate made before the Civil War than any other college. The hall is remarkable for its elaborately carved hammer-beam roof, and the library has richly carved doors, a notable plaster frieze and sixteenth-century cases for its books. There was a little new building, including a house for the President up to the beginning of the seventeenth century and no more until after the Restoration when the most important additions were those made by President Thomas Turner, who left his mark on the college with those which he erected at his own expense.

THE LIBRARY

CORPUS CHRISTI COLLEGE   The photograph illustrates how the pillar, surmounted by a square-faced perpetual calendar, and above that a sun-dial, dominates the front quadrangle.

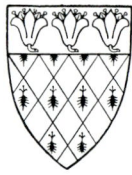

MAGDALEN COLLEGE

For more than five centuries the graceful tower of Magdalen College has been one of Oxford's most famous—and most beautiful landmarks. In its setting of river and meadow against a background of tree-lined hills, it is approached by the bridge which bears the same name and marks the beginning of High Street which leads into the centre of the city. The tower crowns the college which commemorates a Lincolnshire man, William of Waynflete, Bishop of Winchester and Lord Chancellor of England who, in 1448, was given a licence to found a hall for the study of theology and philosophy, on a site between the present Examination Schools and Logic Lane. In 1456, when he became Lord Chancellor, King Henry VI granted him the Hospital of St. John the Baptist, which stood just outside the east gate of the city, and two years later a Charter was given to the College of St. Mary Magdalen; accordingly the year 1458 is traditionally accepted as its foundation date. At first the hospital buildings served for the purposes of the new college, and some of the ancient walls are still preserved in the block of buildings between the entrance gate and the tower, while the college kitchens near the river may have served a similar purpose for the earlier institution. Behind the gateway is St. John's Quadrangle, the centre of the college, with the Founder's Tower, the Muniment Tower and chapel and, as one of its most notable features, the open-air pulpit from which a sermon is preached every year.

The tower was begun in 1492 and took seventeen years to complete, probably because funds ran out from time to time. The chapel suffered in the Reformation, but is still one of the most beautiful in Oxford and is particularly rich in adornments, such as the painting above the altar of Christ carrying the Cross by a Spanish artist, which is said to have been looted by the Duke of Ormonde. The hall, approached by a steep staircase from the cloisters, is a splendid chamber with panelled walls, a Jacobean screen and a notable collection of portraits of Magdalen men through the ages—among them two Cardinals, Wolsey who was once Bursar and Pole, Prince Rupert and the venerable Dr. Routh, who was President for 63 years until he died on the eve of his hundredth birthday. No college has more beautiful grounds, especially the Water Walks with their carpet of fritillaries in early spring, and the Grove with its herd of deer which has been there since the early days of the eighteenth century. The college dines off venison once a year on Restoration Day, but it no longer comes from its own animals, which are carefully tended by a member of the staff. The bridge, built two hundred years ago and widened in 1882, is crowded each May Morning when, from the top of the tower the choir heralds the spring with a Latin hymn.

MAGDALEN COLLEGE—The Hall

MAGDALEN COLLEGE DEER PARK

A herd of deer has been one of the attractions of Magdalen College for about two hundred and fifty years. They are purely decorative and the venison for the traditional Restoration Dinner each year comes from elsewhere.

MANSFIELD COLLEGE

Mansfield College has the distinction of being the first centre of education for members of the Free Churches to be founded in Oxford after religious tests were abolished by Act of Parliament in 1871, which allowed Nonconformists to take degrees at the University except for those in theology. Built originally for Congregationalists, it occupies one of the most attractive of all college sites, and one which still retains much of the rural charm it enjoyed when the first show of the Royal Agricultural Society of England was held there in 1839—an event commemorated by a mulberry tree planted in the garden by the late Princess Royal more than a century later. The original buildings were opened in 1889, and in 1962, seven years after it had been granted the status of a Permanent Private Hall, Queen Elizabeth the Queen Mother opened extensions which completed the traditional Oxford quadrangle and provided extra accommodation for the growing number of students. Through the years Mansfield has sent ordinands, not only to the Free Churches in Britain, but to many churches overseas and to the Anglican Church in America.

LINCOLN COLLEGE

Henry VI was an infant when he granted, in 1427, the Charter for the 'collegiolum', or 'little college', which Richard Fleming, Bishop of the vast diocese of Lincoln, which stretched from the Humber to the Thames, founded in Oxford to combat the heretical teachings of the Lollards, the followers of John Wycliffe. Its aim was to be, he said, in the language of Christian charity which distinguished the times, "to defend the mysteries of the sacred page against those ignorant laics who profaned with swinish snouts, its most holy pearls" and to emphasise the point he later dug up Wycliffe's bones and threw them into a neighbouring river. He endowed his college of 'The Blessed Mary and All Saints Lincoln' with the revenues of three local churches, St. Michael's, All Saints and St. Mildred's, the last of which was demolished, and its site used for the first buildings of the new foundation. The front quadrangle, particularly when its creeper-covered walls glow scarlet in the late summer, is one of the most attractive in Oxford, and the greater part was built through the munificence of Dean Forrest of Wells, a few years after the founder's death in 1431. One of its chief glories is the hall, perfectly proportioned, with its original roof, complete with louvre or smoke hole through which escaped the smoke from the fire which was kindled on the hearthstone which still remains in the floor. The chapel is another architectural gem, with its beautiful woodwork and its open timber roof, resplendent with armorial bearings and other devices. The most renowned of all Lincoln's sons is, of course, John Wesley, the founder of Methodism, who was a Fellow of the College for 25 years until he married. His room has been carefully preserved, enriched by the lovely sixteenth-century linenfold panelling which now lines it—the gift of American Methodists nearly fifty years ago.

THE COLLEGE HALL
The hall of Lincoln is the oldest surviving college hall in Oxford to retain its original (fifteenth-century) roof.

29

CHRIST CHURCH

Christ Church, or 'the House' as it is more familiarly known by its members, was first conceived by Thomas Wolsey, Cardinal of York, reminders of whom are to be found everywhere about it. In 1524, the Pope gave him permission to dissolve the ancient Priory of St. Frideswide, and a little later to suppress a score of monasteries so that he should have the land and the money to found a college in Oxford which was to outdo in mangificence any other. Accordingly, on a July day in the following year, the foundation stone of Cardinal College was laid by the Bishop of Lincoln, and at the same time the Cardinal issued his foundation Charter. The new college was to be on an unprecedented scale, and building had actually begun before the foundation stone was laid. Thousands of pounds were lavished on the work, and a small army of workmen was engaged in fulfilling Wolsey's designs, but everything came to a standstill when he fell into disgrace with his master the King. At first it was thought that Henry would demolish those buildings which had been erected, but eventually, in July 1532, the college was re-founded as 'King Henry VIII College', but this had only been in existence for thirteen years when it was followed by a third creation, in which the Cathedral, formerly at Osney, and the college were united as 'The Cathedral Church of Christ in Oxford'. And so Christ Church has been styled ever since. Although the dreams of its first founder were never realised, it is the largest and most splendid of all the colleges in the university, with its unique chapel which is also the mother church of the Oxford Diocese.

Its magnificent hall and the imposing stairway leading to it, its huge kitchen still retaining some of its original equipment, its old library and the newer, splendid building which houses an incomparable collection of books and manuscripts—Wolsey's own service book among them—are outstanding features. Tom Tower, over the main gate, was designed by Sir Christopher Wren and houses 'Great Tom', brought from Osney Abbey and later re-cast, which still booms out 101 strokes every night. The hall is breath-taking in its splendour, 115 ft. long, 40 ft. wide and 50 ft. high, crowned with a richly ornamented roof, the walls covered by as many as space allows of the three hundred portraits which the college owns. But perhaps the crowning glory of Christ Church is the Meadow, south of its buildings, in which cattle graze within almost a stone's throw of the centre of Oxford.

CHRIST CHURCH STAIRWAY
The magnificent stairway leading to the hall at Christ Church was built by Samuel Fell, Dean 1638-1648.

CHRIST CHURCH MEMORIAL GARDEN

A block of old and decaying buildings was swept away to provide a site for a memorial to those members of the House who gave their lives in the First World War—a lovely place of close-mown lawns, herbaceous borders and rose beds against grey stone walls.

THE LAW LIBRARY

The Law Library in its semi-rural setting, is an important addition to Oxford's architecture, and the massive building which houses it is shared also by the English faculty and the Institute of Economics and Statistics. It consists of a complex of libraries, lecture rooms and offices, each self-contained, but sharing a common entrance hall and other facilities. Provision for the university's collection of law books became urgent after the war, for the existing accommodation was inadequate, and in addition there was a considerable increase in the number of law students at the university. The Rockefeller Foundation gave £150,000, more than half the estimated cost of the new building and work on it began in 1959, and it was opened in October 1964 by Dean Griswold, head of the Harvard Law School. It provides space for 450,000 books and 320 Readers, a common room for members of the law faculty and a coffee bar for undergraduates.

THE CATHEDRAL

The Cathedral Church of Christ in Oxford is unique. Not only is it the smallest, and one of the most charming of all English cathedrals, but it is also a college chapel. Its story goes back for more than a thousand years to the days of the Saxons and embraces the Danish invaders, the Normans and those who succeeded them, but it will always be associated with a Princess who became a saint—Frideswide or Fritheswith—'the bond of peace'. The daughter of a minor monarch who ruled the Oxford district under the kingdom of Mercia, she vowed her life to God. Her father built a small church in one of the most pleasant spots in his domain, among meadows surrounded by meandering streams and against a background of wooded hills. She who was to become a saint and Patroness of Oxford, both city and university, founded a nunnery, which was not to survive for long. Nor did her father's church, which was burned to the ground on St. Brice's day, 1002, after it had been used as a refuge by Danes seeking to escape the massacre ordered by Ethelred the Unready. The king rebuilt the church on a larger scale and after the Normans came, the nunnery became a house of the Canons Regular of St. Augustine; there was another restoration and the church was again enlarged.

In the centuries which followed there were further changes. Every period of English medieval Gothic is represented in the lovely building and the steeple is believed to be the first ever built in this country. Cardinal Wolsey would have destroyed St. Frideswide's when he built his new college, but he fell into disgrace and his work was halted. It was only a century ago that the western end, walled off and built up by Wolsey, was reconstructed and opened, to give an entrance into the main quadrangle of Christ Church. The east end of the choir is not Norman but nineteenth-century rebuilding, and the window over the altar is a reproduction of twelfth century craftsmanship.

CHRIST CHURCH—Seen from the famous Meadow.

LINACRE COLLEGE

Late in 1977, the college moved into its present home at the junction of South Parks Road and St Cross Road, after conversions and additions to a large house known as Cherwell Edge. This was a private house from its building in 1886–7 until 1905, when it became a convent which for many years housed women undergraduates, mainly from the Society of Home Students – which in turn became St Anne's College. Linacre was established in 1962 as a society for men and women graduates reading for advanced degrees and diplomas. It was first housed in St Aldate's, in the buildings occupied by the former St Catherine's Society. About half of its students are from overseas. One of the new features of the college is its dining hall, but in addition, considerable alterations were made inside the house, including provision of a library and common room. The college is perhaps, the most strategically placed of all Oxford colleges. It is close to the Science Area, and to the University Parks and the beautiful stretch of open space known as Mesopotamia. Its financial future has been made more secure by the provision of a £1m endowment fund. The money is to be provided from the College Contributions Fund, set up in 1967, under which the richer colleges undertook to establish such funds for their poorer neighbours. But the college has also been greatly helped by gifts and benefactions from trusts and foundations at home and abroad.

ST HILDA'S COLLEGE

St Hilda's was the last of the women's colleges to be founded. It dates from 1893 when Miss Dorothy Beale, Principal of Cheltenham Ladies' College, bought Cowley House, not far from Magdalen Bridge, and converted it into a hall where promising students from Cheltenham could spend an extra year in higher education, attending lectures and receiving tuition. A former Principal is on record as saying that the college 'is the first on the left as you come into Oxford from the London direction'. So it is, but it is tucked away in what used to be the Milham Ford area. It started off with seven students and the number had only grown to 12 by 1896, but the growing pressure for women to enter the University after the first World War led to the beginning of a scheme of expansion which has resulted in St Hilda's now possessing a fine range of buildings, some of them of fairly recent origin, on one of the most beautiful sites in Oxford. The gardens slope down to the River Cherwell, there is a long river frontage, and the grounds provide a fine view of Oxford across Christ Church Meadow, which is much appreciated by the many visitors attending conferences in the college during the Long Vacation.

MERTON COLLEGE   The chapel, with its beautiful tower, is among the remains of the original buildings.

MERTON COLLEGE

'The House of the Scholars of Merton' takes its name, as its founder did, from the old Augustinian Priory of Merton in Surrey. Walter de Merton, Bishop of Rochester and sometime Lord High Chancellor of England, gave his estates to provide an income for the support of eight young kinsmen—they were his nephews, sons of his five sisters— to study at Oxford where he himself had been a student. A little later, he increased the number of students to twenty, including some who were not relatives, and in 1266 bought some property in a street which took its name from the local parish church of St. John the Baptist, from the Abbot of Reading. The Statutes, which he drew up for governing his foundation, laid down every detail of life as it was to be lived there; they remained in force for nearly five hundred years—until 1856. It was 'the first great permanent endowment of learning in England', and the original small plot of land was extended by the acquisition of the little church of St. John and a number of adjoining properties. In 1290, work on a new church and chapel was begun, and when the choir was completed, the old one was allowed to fall into decay, though it was not until the end of 1425 that the new church was re-dedicated. It remained a parish church until the beginning of the present century, when the living was united with neighbouring St. Peter in the East, which in turn shared the fate of assimilation into a college. Little remains today of the buildings the founder knew, save for the chapel which has been restored and altered from time to time, the ancient carving over the main entrance in Merton Street, the massive door which leads into the hall and, perhaps, the treasury. The rest came into being after his death in 1277. Apart from the chapel, the most outstanding building is the library, the oldest medieval example of its kind in England. Built in the last quarter of the fourteenth century, it has been enriched, improved and adorned in succeeding centuries—beautiful plaster-work and panelling, lovely glass and a sixteenth-century ceiling, but it is still essentially the room in which the scholars of the Middle Ages pored over the manuscripts and the books which were chained to the desks. The library and living rooms, which were built between 1304 and 1309, enclose what is known as Mob Quad, the earliest of all the Oxford quadrangles, which came into being by accident not design. How it got its quaint name nobody knows, and in earlier times it was called the Bachelors' Quadrangle; the Fellows were known as Bachelors. At one time Merton was noted for the number of Bishops it produced, but its alumni include men famous in many fields, particularly science. It also has the distinction of having the only Head of an Oxford college who died in jail. Thomas Reynolds, who became Warden in 1545, was a Tudor Vicar of Bray.

A Protestant when Edward VI was on the throne, he became a chaplain to Queen Mary, and when she died, immediately offered his services to her sister Elizabeth, but with no success. He was deprived of both the Wardenship and the Deanery of Exeter which he also held and was sent to the Marshalsea Prison, where he died. When Oxford was the Royalist head-quarters during the Civil War, Queen Henrietta Maria had her apartments there and a special gateway was opened between Merton and Christ Church where the King stayed. One of the glories of the college is its lovely setting, overlooking Merton Fields, skirted by Dead Man's Walk, called so it is said, because it is haunted by the ghost of a Cavalier officer executed there during the Civil War.

A CHAINED BOOK is treasured in the College's library of magnificently bound volumes.

Oxfords' skyline from the east, some of the beautiful curve of High Street, and the western hills beyond, are seen in this dramatic picture.

THE ENCAENIA

The annual commemoration is the most colourful of all the Universitys' Ceremonies. The leading figures of the University—'Heads of Houses, Doctors, Proctors', and the rest—having partaken of Nathaniel, Lord Crewe's traditional benefaction of strawberries and cream with champagne accompaniment, walk in procession, headed by the Chancellor, to the Sheldonian Theatre for the Encaenia, when benefactors are commemorated and eminent men and women from all over the world are honoured with degrees.

Here the procession is shown passing the Clarendon Building, built by Hawksmoor, which housed the University Press from 1713 to 1829. In latter years it was the administrative headquarters of the University, and is now part of the Bodleian Library.

TRINITY COLLEGE

Trinity College, with its lovely gardens and Balliol and St. John's as neighbours, has its roots in the thirteenth-century foundation of Durham College, established by Benedictine monks. The old buildings, derelict and ruinous, were bought by an Oxfordshire farmer's son who became one of the richest men in England—Sir Thomas Pope, who is buried in the chapel of his college, Letters Patent for which were dated March 8, 1555. Some of the older buildings are incorporated in those he built, which comprise three quadrangles, with other extensions added in the years since the last war. Everywhere are lawns, trees and borders of flowers which can be viewed through iron gates and grilles, the most impressive glimpse being that of the garden front from Parks Road. At the main gate is an attractive range of seventeenth-century cottages, recently restored and beyond them, Kettell Hall which commemorates the name of Dr. Ralph Kettell, an eccentric seventeenth-century President. The chapel, which replaces an earlier building, was consecrated in 1694. It is a beautiful place, with a rich plaster ceiling and, above all, the Grinling Gibbons carving—screen, altar rails, reredos and stalls all showing the inimitable touch of the master hand. The hall, newly decorated, is another gem of Stuart Gothic; its cellars have become an undergraduate meeting place.

GREEN COLLEGE

Oxford's medical school, which came into being through the generosity of Lord Nuffield, has become world-famous. Now the University has a college devoted to the interests of clinical medical students, and again a private benefactor has made it possible. Green College, the University's youngest foundation, came into being chiefly through a gift in 1977 of £1m by Dr Cecil H. Green, founder-director of Texas Instruments Inc., and his wife Ida, who live in Dallas, Texas. Later they added another £29,000, and finally gave £817,000 to ensure that the planned building programme would be carried through quickly. A range of buildings was designed to merge unobtrusively with the 18th century architecture already on the site. They incorporate the famous Radcliffe Observatory with its Tower of Winds – which has been painstakingly restored – built in 1794, and described by Sir Nikolaus Pevsner as 'architecturally the finest observatory in Europe'. For many years the Tower and its lovely buildings have been obscured by a clutter of unsightly huts which had to be built to meet the growing needs of the nearby Radcliffe Infirmary. The entrance lodge in Woodstock Road, surmounted by a cupola holding a four-faced clock, in itself a handsome addition to this part of Oxford.

ST ANTONY'S COLLEGE

The college, which is next door to St Anne's in the Woodstock Road, occupies a somewhat gaunt building which was once a convent, but since it opened its doors in 1950, some outstanding examples of modern architecture have been added to it. St Antony's came into being as a result of a benefaction from the late M. Antonin Besse of Aden, and his gift and his wishes about the use to which it should be put were kept closely guarded secrets for some 18 months before they were announced. It is a graduate college, with an international and distinguished membership. From the outset it was planned as a centre for advanced study and research in the fields of modern international history, economics and politics, and to provide an international centre within the University where students from all over the world could live and work together in close contact with senior members of the University who were specialists in their fields. Apart from European Studies, the college established a number of regional centres concerned with the study of the problems of the Middle East, Latin America, the Far East, including Japan, Russia, Eastern Europe and Africa.

ST HUGH'S COLLEGE

St Hugh's was established as St Hugh's Hall in 1886 by Dame Elizabeth Wordsworth, the first Principal of Lady Margaret Hall. It was intended for those who could not afford the fees at Lady Margaret Hall, and was named after St Hugh of Lincoln, of which Miss Wordsworth's father was Bishop. Its beginnings were modest in the extreme – four students and a capital endowment of £600. It had to struggle, more than the other women's colleges for many years, in the face of growing need for more buildings and to meet the pressing demands for more places for women at Oxford. But eventually, it was helped by many generous benefactors. Its first home was in a house in Norham Gardens, and it was another 40 years before it began to acquire its own buildings. Its buildings grew more slowly than those of other colleges because its finances were so inadequate. But at the beginning of the 1914–18 war, it became possible at last to secure part of the present site, bounded to the east and west by Banbury Road and Woodstock Road and to north and south by St Margaret's Road and Canterbury Road. The next 40 years were marked by steady growth, and the whole of the island site of 14 acres, which provide a college campus as fine as any in Oxford was acquired. Like the other women's colleges, St Hugh's owes much to the generosity, not only of its old members, but to the Wolfson Foundation which gave each of them £100,000. Nowadays, the college is able to house all but a few of its members, both undergraduate and graduate, in its own residential accommodation.

ST ANNE'S COLLEGE

The University education of women in Oxford began with the founding of the Association for the Education of Women in 1878. Included among the women the Association admitted were some, from the first, who preferred to live at home. That was the origin of the first title of the college – the Society of Oxford Home Students, which gave place in turn to St Anne's Society and eventually to St Anne's College. It has, in the words of the Principal 'floated' until today it occupies a commanding site in the triangle formed by the Woodstock and Banbury roads, with its base in Bevington Road. The headquarters of the college moved in turn from the home of the first Principal in South Parks Road to Jowett Walk, in a few rooms at the back of the School of Geography building, then to Musgrave House (now the Department of Theoretical Chemistry). Then a benefaction from Mrs Amy Hartland made possible the erection of the first new building on the present site for a library. The college has gone on from there, and along both the Woodstock and Banbury Roads, there are buildings which have been recognised as outstanding examples of modern architecture.

The college was granted full college status in the University in 1959 – a complete transformation from the time when women were admitted to higher education only on sufferance – because of the enlightened attitude of many Oxford dons, and, as a writer has said 'the major discovery of the 19th century that women have brains'.

SOMERVILLE COLLEGE

The college has produced a host of women famous in many fields, among them Britain's first woman Prime Minister. It was where Dorothy Sayers was taught, and most of the visitors to Somerville want to see her room. It is her admirers who ask the college librarian for information about her, both personally and in letters. Dorothy Sayers was at Somerville from 1912 to 1914. Mrs Gandhi was at Somerville, and in the learned field, perhaps the most famous former student is Prof Dorothy Hodgkin, who won the Nobel Prize for Chemistry.

Somerville is junior by a whisker to Lady Margaret Hall. It is remaining single-sex. The presence of students of many nationalities is a feature of the college; it received the first five women Rhodes Scholars in 1977, and seven of the second batch the following year. Somerville was founded as an undenominational college. It opened on the same day, October 13 1879, as Lady Margaret Hall, which was a Church of England foundation. The split between Church of England and undenominational views had by then widened beyond repair. The name Somerville was given to the new hall in honour of Mary Somerville who, on her death in 1872 was acclaimed the queen of 19th century science, and the founders declared their intention that the new society would not confine its scope to the humanities – this at a time when the place of science in education, even for men, was minimal.

The college has a modest entrance in the Woodstock Road, but it now occupies a large site between that road and Walton Street. Here again, the gardens are a notable feature.

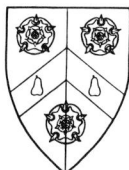

WOLFSON COLLEGE

Wolfson College stands, a longish way from the rest of Oxford's colleges, on a beautiful site on the edge of the River Cherwell, as a remarkable monument to the outstanding generosity of the Wolfson and Ford Foundations. The former gave a grant of £1½m. for the buildings and the latter an equal sum for the endowment of the college. It is a graduate college, and came into being as an answer to two seemingly intractable problems facing the University. Many of its academic staff, especially in the natural sciences, had no part in the life of the colleges, and there was difficulty in providing for the ever growing number of graduate students. Wolfson incorporates Iffley College which had been founded in 1965 as part of Oxford's response to those who had no college fellowships. It is probably Oxford's most egalitarian college, and was conceived as a single community with minimal distinctions of status. The single Common Room and all the facilities of the college are open to all members of the college, to their wives and to the administrative and secretarial staff. Graduate students sit on all college committees except those concerned with the selection or tenure of individual Fellows, students or members of staff. The college houses the Centre for Socio-Legal Studies. The foundation stone of the college was laid by the Queen on May 2 1968, and building started in October 1969.

WORCESTER COLLEGE

Although Worcester College (opposite page) was founded only in 1714, it has a continuous history as an academic institution in the University which goes back for nearly seven centuries. It was in 1283 that Sir John Giffard bought Gloucester Hall, a private house adjoining the royal palace of Beaumont, and gave it to the Benedictines of the Abbey of St. Peter, Gloucester, as "a nursery and mansion place" for their novices. Later, students from other Benedictine Abbeys in the Province of Canterbury joined them, the buildings were enlarged, and eventually fifteen abbeys were sending young men to be educated there. They were housed in chambers like the picturesque 'cottages' which still survive on the south side of the front quadrangle of the present college, and the abbeys to which these belonged can still be identified by their arms over the entrances. At the Dissolution of the monasteries, the supply of students ceased, and the old monastic buildings were given by the king to the new See of Oxford which he had created, as a residence for the Bishop, but if Richard King, last Abbot of Osney and first Bishop of Oxford, occupied them, it was only for a short time. In 1560, Gloucester College, or what remained of it, was acquired by Sir Thomas White, founder of St. John's College, and leased to one of the Fellows to become Gloucester Hall. As such it continued with varying fortunes; towards the end of the seventeenth century one Principal tried to turn it into a college for theological students of the Greek Church. The money to establish the new foundation and endow it came from a bequest in the will of a Worcestershire baronet, Sir Thomas Cookes, and he was followed by other benefactors, notably Dr. George Clarke, a Fellow of All Souls. The college is particularly noted for its lovely garden, in which is a lake.

The ornamental lake, which attracts, as well as swans, a wide variety of wildfowl.

ST. JOHN'S COLLEGE

Another victim of the Dissolution of the Monasteries in Oxford was St. Bernard's College, the ruins of which were acquired by Sir Thomas White, a London merchant and a leading member of the Merchant Taylors' Company. There is a charming story that he was guided by a dream, in which he saw ancient buildings with a row of elms at their side, to St. Bernard's, which was to become his college, planned under the protection of St. John the Baptist, patron saint of tailors. He bought the ruins in 1555, and on them built his new foundation, the first members of which came into residence two years later. When the Merchant Taylors' School was established a little later some places in the new college were reserved for its boys, a connection which has lasted to the present day. Outside the entrance in St. Giles is a tree-shaded terrace which has been there certainly since Elizabethan days, and the front quadrangle consists largely of the buildings of the original home of the monks of the Cistercian Order, who were sent to Oxford to study. The gate tower, adorned with statues, including one of St. Bernard, opens into a quadrangle which contains the President's residence, the chapel and the hall, converted from the old kitchens of the monastic establishment.

THE FRONT QUADRANGLE

THE CANTERBURY QUADRANGLE

Beyond lies the Canterbury Quadrangle, with its two loggias and two libraries, almost entirely the creation of Archbishop Laud, one of St. John's most distinguished sons, who was to perish on the scaffold and whose poignant relics are among the most treasured possessions of the college. Another eminent churchman, Archbishop Juxon, who attended King Charles at his execution, succeeded Laud as President. The hall, which had been the scene of Royal revels in Stuart times, was considerably altered in the eighteenth century, and the chapel, since it was first consecrated, underwent many changes, chiefly under Laud's direction. To it for burial Archbishop Laud's body was brought eighteen years after his death, but the only memorial in the college is a coffin plate. One of the loveliest features of St. John's is its famous rock garden, a monument to Henry Jardine Bidder, Fellow and Keeper of the Groves, who made it.

UNIVERSITY COLLEGE

The story that University College was founded by Alfred the Great is a pleasant fiction, although celebrations were held in 1872 to 'commemorate' the thousandth year of its foundation by that remarkable king. It derives its origin from a benefaction of William of Durham, a prominent medieval cleric who died in 1249, leaving to the university the sum of 310 marks to buy property, the income from which was to be devoted to the maintenance of a number of needy Masters of Arts who were studying divinity. This was done within a few years, and the houses bought were on the opposite side of High Street from the present buildings of the college. Thirty years later questions were being asked about the money, obviously with some effect, for a document written in 1280 lays down the rules for the foundation of a new college—a small one since its members numbered only four. This was the beginning of 'the College of the Great Hall of the University', now one of the largest in Oxford, with an imposing frontage in High Street more than 400 ft. long. In the fifteenth century there was a wide range of buildings, but the medieval quadrangle was swept away two hundred years later in a wholesale rebuilding scheme. Its successors represent the Gothic tradition from the seventeenth to the twentieth centuries. The main gateway, under a battlemented tower, leads into the larger quadrangle, with the chapel and hall in the range opposite the entrance. Building was interrupted by the Civil War and it was not until 1669 that the whole was completed.

Dr. John Radcliffe, an old member and one of Oxford's most munificent benefactors, left £5,000 to the college for building purposes, and the money was used to buy a new quadrangle which is named after him. The tower over the gate leading from the street, has on one side a statue of Queen Mary II, and on the other, one of the doctor himself, while his arms are carved—with those of the college—on the vaulting. The hall stands above a vaulted cellar and has a fine roof, long hidden by plaster, and walls adorned with portraits of famous members of the college, the work of equally eminent artists. Other buildings were added in the nineteenth and again in this century; one of the most famous is the domed chamber containing the memorial to the poet Shelley.

RADCLIFFE QUADRANGLE
The Radcliffe Quadrangle, at University College is a memorial to Dr. John Radcliffe who bequeathed the money for its construction. On the left is the gateway with its vaulted ceiling, seen from the High, which leads from the busy street into the tranquillity of a lovely quadrangle.

THE UNIVERSITY CHURCH
OF ST. MARY THE VIRGIN

The unusual twisted columns ("like barley sugar sticks") of the porch which forms the main entrance to the Church of St. Mary the Virgin which is second in size only to the cathedral. It has also a two-fold purpose; not only is it a parish church, though with a tiny resident population these days, but it is the university church as well. It was for centuries the heart of the university, housing the first library as well as the university chest; it was the central meeting place for masters and scholars, the courthouse where delinquents were held for trial and punishment, where academical disputations took place and degrees were conferred. The present lovely building, the greater part of which was built in the fifteenth century, is the third church to occupy the site, and there is still much within its walls that is far older.

KEBLE COLLEGE

A striking contrast in architectural styles is provided by two buildings, separated in age by only a century, Keble College and the University Law Library. The college was built as a memorial to the Rev. John Keble, one of the founders of the Tractarian Movement which was to transform the Church of England in the nineteenth century, to make "all the academical and other privileges of Oxford life accessible to men of limited means and also maintain the traditional association of the University with the Church of England". A public appeal for funds was made after Keble's death, and the results were so successful that the college was able to open in 1870, although the buildings were not finally completed until twelve years later. They were a revolution as far as an Oxford college was concerned, with red brick walls, striped and chequered with black, and with some bands and all the dressings carried out in light-coloured stone, a feature characteristic of the architect, William Butterfield. Hands were raised in horror at such an intrusion amidst Oxford stone and it is said that as a result Ruskin never again walked in the Parks as was his invariable custom when he was in Oxford, because he could not bear the sight of the new building. The interior arrangement of rooms was also a new departure. Instead of the traditional staircase giving access to two sets of rooms on each floor, the rooms themselves of a more modest size were approached by passages. The great quadrangle and its lovely lawns, is dominated by the chapel with its lofty tower, a splendid example of its kind, notable, above all for Holman Hunt's painting of 'The Light of the World'. The artist fifty years later produced the copy which hangs in St. Paul's Cathedral. The hall is the longest in the university, 3 ft. more than that of Christ Church but it is not so wide or so lofty, nor can it claim to be as beautiful, and the range of buildings which includes the library is beautifully proportioned.

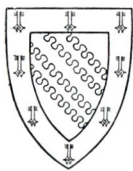

EXETER COLLEGE

Exeter, the fourth oldest of the Oxford colleges, was founded by a Bishop who was murdered by a London mob. Walter de Stapledon, Bishop of Exeter between 1307 and 1326, a notable benefactor both to his diocese and to Devon, in 1314 established what was to be known as Stapledon Hall in Hart Hall, but the following year he moved his twelve scholars into tenements he had bought just within the city walls, which still form part of the site of the present college. Of this original band of scholars eight were from Devon and four from Cornwall, establishing a strong west country connection between the two which is still maintained. Exeter was practically refounded in 1566 by Sir William Petre, another benefactor who had been Secretary of State to three Tudor sovereigns. Nothing remains of the pre-Reformation college except the tower in the north-east corner of the quadrangle, built in 1432, the base of which was the original gateway, leading into a narrow lane which has long since disappeared. The rest of the buildings date from the seventeenth and nineteenth centuries. The hall, built in 1618, is one of the loveliest of the smaller college halls, and the money was provided by Sir John Acland, whose coat of arms adorns the richly-wrought screen. The magnificent timbered roof is of Spanish chestnut and there is a number of interesting portraits, including one of King Charles I, who was another benefactor. The chapel, which is based on La Saint Chapelle in Paris, was designed by Sir Gilbert Scott in the 1850 s. It contains a piece of tapestry representing the Adoration of the Magi, which was designed by Burne-Jones and executed by William Morris, both of whom were undergraduates at the college.

EXETER COLLEGE HALL

PEMBROKE COLLEGE

"Sir, we are a nest of singing birds" Dr. Samuel Johnson told Boswell in a reference to his old college Pembroke where he went as an undergraduate in 1728, just over a century after it had been founded. The college still treasures the famous blue and white teapot, with a capacity of half a gallon, which belonged to the famous man. It was on June 29, 1624, that James I issued Letters Patent creating the new foundation of Pembroke College, the direct descendant of Broadgates, one of the leading medieval academic halls. Although the king was pleased to style himself the Founder, the honour really belonged to two more humble benefactors, Thomas Tesdale, a wealthy maltster of Abingdon and the Rev. Richard Wightwicke, Rector of East Ilsley. Dr. Clayton, the last principal of Broadgates became the first Master of Pembroke and the charming front quadrangle, gay in summer with its flower-laden window boxes, was built between 1624 and 1670. The entrance in the cobbled square was added towards the end of the same century and the chapel dates from 1728. Beef Lane, named after another ancient hall, and the houses on the south side of Pembroke Street, were incorporated in the college to make a most charming quadrangle, after the last war.

ST CROSS COLLEGE

St Cross College was founded in 1965 as one of the few colleges in the University of Oxford specially for graduate students. At present there are some 75 fellows (senior members of the University teaching staff) and 115 students (studying for research degrees and postgraduate diplomas of the University).

The main centre of the College is in St Giles, in the heart of Oxford, where it occupies a distinguished stone building designed by the Victorian architect Temple Moore.

THE OXFORD CENTRE FOR ISLAMIC STUDIES

The Oxford Centre for Islamic Studies was established in October 1985 by the Islamic Trust to promote an understanding of Islam through advanced research, teaching and co-operation between Muslim and non-Muslim scholars and academic institutions. It aims to sponsor its own research programmes which will be concerned not only with religious, cultural and historical aspects of Islam, but equally with the relevance of modern advances in science technology, medicine and economics.

Among the means of achieving these aims, the founding Trustees have placed particular emphasis on the provision of visiting Fellowships and Scholarships to promote academic collaboration in various Universities and on the maximum practical co-operation with the University of Oxford, and a close association with St Cross College, where the Centre is based.

ST CROSS COLLEGE
Richard Blackwell Quadrangle

PEMBROKE COLLEGE   The college takes great pride in its window boxes. These are in the inner quadrangle, and at the height of their glory.

ST. CATHERINE'S COLLEGE

A few hours after the Queen had laid the foundation stone of St. Catherine's College on November 4, 1960, three members of the college were discovered by the police (who had been tipped off) removing it in the wheelbarrow. It was recovered, slightly damaged, and the miscreants were rusticated—sent home—for a few weeks, to be pardoned when they had made suitable apologies. The college began as a non-collegiate body of students, in 1868, which in 1930 was re-named St. Catherine's Society; after the saint and martyr who is the patron of learning. The buildings were designed by the Danish architect, Arne Jacobsen, whose commission extended to the gardens, the furniture and even the college plate—a unique distinction. The cost was nearly £3 million and the money came from industry and commerce, charitable foundations and a number of private benefactors.

ORIEL COLLEGE

Although the ill-fated King Edward II is claimed as the founder of Oriel College, it was actually founded by an astute medieval cleric, Adam de Brome, his Almoner who, in 1324, acquired two properties for a proposed society of scholars which was to be called 'The College of St. Mary in Oxford'. However two years later he surrendered these possessions to his royal master, who re-established the society with Adam de Brome as its first Provost. Among the houses which the new college possessed was one called La Oriole, which stood on the site of the present main quadrangle, and was obviously the origin of the name of the new foundation. During the Middle Ages and the sixteenth century, a number of buildings had grown up round the hall, but by the beginning of the seventeenth century they had proved inadequate for the growing needs of the college and the task of rebuilding began in 1619, to be completed with the chapel more than thirty years later. Since then there have been further extensions and there are now three quadrangles which extend from High Street to Merton Street. Many famous men have been associated with Oriel including two famous adventurers whose exploits are separated by nearly three centuries—Sir Walter Raleigh and Cecil Rhodes.

BRASENOSE COLLEGE

'The King's Hall and Brasenose College' takes its quaint name from the thirteenth-century hall, from which it is directly descended, and after its unusual and conspicuous knocker—the bronze head of a lion or leopard, pierced with a large ring, which remains one of the oldest and most prized treasures of the college. It had two founders, William Smyth, Bishop of Lincoln, and Richard Sutton, a lawyer, both of whom were in the service of King Henry VII. The bishop provided for the cost of the building, and the lawyer acquired the property for the site, and the new college received its charter on January 15, 1512. It has one of the most distinguished settings of any in the academic centre of Oxford in Radcliffe Square surrounded by other famous centres of piety and learning. The front quadrangle, which is of particular charm, was built by 1516 with the dormer windows added later in the reign of James I. The hall, also built in the sixteenth century has been altered, both inside and out, in the intervening centuries, and the chapel which dates from the second half of the seventeenth century, replaces the undistinguished original on the first floor of the range which includes the hall. Alexander Nowell, who was Principal at the end of the sixteenth century is credited with the invention of bottled beer; after leaving a bottle of ale buried in the ground, he retrieved it later to discover that it was "not a bottle but a gun, such the sound of it when it opened". Brasenose has also interesting links with the United States for the for bears of two Presidents were undergraduates there—Laurence Washington, great-grandfather of George and the Rev. Thomas Adams who was the grandfather of John Adams.

The High Street frontage.

THE QUEEN'S COLLEGE

Oxford's famous High Street—'The High' as it is universally known—with its graceful curves and lines with splendid buildings in infinite variety, has been called the loveliest street in Europe. Two of its dominating features are the imposing facade of the Queen's College founded in 1341 by Robert d' Eglesfield, Chaplain of Queen Philippa, wife of Edward III, and the university church of St. Mary the Virgin. Eglesfield's aim was to increase the number of learned clergy, especially in his native county of Cumberland, and adjoining Westmorland, a connection with the north country which remains to this day. The college was also to be a charitable centre. Pea soup was to be distributed as its gates, and unfortunates, such as the blind, deaf and dumb and cripples, were to be entertained daily in its hall. Other rules were that the scholars were to be summoned to their meals by trumpet, a custom which is still observed, and Queen's was also to brew its own ale. Like the distribution of soup and the daily entertainment of the poor, this is no longer carried out. The Queen-consort was to be the Patroness, a tradition which is still continued. Originally the main frontage of the college was in Queen's Lane, but in the eighteenth century the medieval buildings were swept away, and the massive facade in the Palladian style, erected in their place. Underneath the cupola over the gateway is a statue of Queen Caroline, wife of George II, who contributed generously to the work.

JESUS COLLEGE

There is an old story concerning Jesus known as the 'Welsh College' of the man who went into the front quadrangle and shouted 'Jones' whereupon every window was flung open and a head popped out. It was the first college to be founded in Oxford after the Reformation and Letters Patent were issued by Queen Elizabeth in June, 1571 at the request of Dr. Hugh Price, son of a Welsh butcher, which provided for a society of eight Fellows and eight scholars, with a Principal. It was to be known as "Jesus College . . . of Queen Elizabeth's foundation". The early years of the new foundation were a struggle, chiefly because of financial difficulties, for although there were buildings there was little, if any, revenue and often insufficient money available to pay its members. Queen Elizabeth who is described in the Benefactors' Book, as "foundresse", gave not only the land for the first buildings, but also timber from the royal forests of Shotover and Stowood. Her portrait hangs in the hall together with others of a notable collection which includes those of Charles I, by Vandyk, Charles II attributed to Lely, and that of Dr. Price which is of the Holbein School. Among other possessions of the college is a watch which once belonged to Charles I, who was an early benefactor, a ring containing his miniature which was worn by his Consort, and a massive silver punchbowl, the largest in Oxford, capable of holding ten gallons!

BALLIOL COLLEGE

The story of Balliol College begins with John de Balliol, Lord of Barnard Castle who had, about the year 1260 not only "unjustly vexed and enormously damnified the Church of Tynemouth and the Church of Durham", but also laid hands on the Bishop.

He was, as a result publicly scourged by the Bishop at the door of Durham Cathedral and ordered to do penance by providing a hostel at Oxford for sixteen poor scholars and pay for their maintenance. By June, 1266, Balliol's first scholars were in residence at the University, lodged in a house facing the moat and city wall in what is now Broad Street, where the main entrance to the famous college still is. Unfortunately, Balliol died three years later, before he could ensure the permanent endowment of his proteges, and it was his widow, Devorguilla who carried on the work he had begun. The earliest of the buildings which survive the changes of the centuries are relics of the first quadrangle, built in the fifteenth century, but of the rest the oldest are only just over a hundred years old, including the chapel which contains some of the sixteenth century stained glass from its predecessor. John Wycliffe the reformer, Cardinal Morton, John Evelyn the diarist, Smith of 'Wealth of Nations' fame, and Southey the poet, are among Balliol's early sons, but it was in the nineteenth century, particularly with the great Dr. Jowett as Master, that the college reached the height of its fame.

The Broad Street frontage, once scorned by architects, but now regarded as a good example of its kind.

THE GOLDEN HEART OF OXFORD

SCIENCE AREA

Scientists have worked in Oxford since the beginning of the 13th century. During the Middle Ages mathematics flourished, as did medicine, although not in the form we know it today. Nonetheless, William Harvey, who came to Oxford in 1642, discovered the circulation of the blood. Astronomers came too—Halley and Bradley among them. During the Civil War, there was a considerable influx of scientists to the University. It was in the early part of the 19th century that science began to boom. At first, some of the colleges established laboratories, and the one at Jesus College, established in 1906, was in constant use until 1947.

Oxford has become renowned as an international scientific centre and spreading from the University Museum and the Clarendon Laboratory, many buildings have been put up to cater for its many facets—low temperature physics, nuclear physics, the discovery of penicillin and cephalosporin, which have saved countless lives, among them.

Most of the new buildings are functional rather than beautiful, but as is shown in this picture of the Biochemistry building, much can be done by planting flowering trees in their surrounds.

LADY MARGARET HALL

L.M.H. – no-one in Oxford uses its full title when speaking of the most senior of the original five women's colleges – was named after Margaret Beaufort, mother of Henry VII. Of her, the founder of the college, Dame Elizabeth Wordsworth, great-niece of the poet, wrote that she was 'a gentlewoman, a scholar and a saint, and after being married three times, she took a vow of celibacy. What more could be expected of any woman?'.

From its modest beginnings in 1878 as the first academic hall for women in Oxford, the college has grown in size and stature. Its first students were lively-minded young women, who scored a first by petitioning the college council for a full-length mirror in the common room, so that they could make sure their appearance was all that it should be when they ventured beyond the college confines – as likely as not accompanied by chaperones. Chaperones have long since disappeared, but the students are just as lively-minded and over the years have made a remarkable contribution to politics, public life, the professions and academic life. The college scored another first in 1979 by appointing a man as its Principal, a move that raised not a few eyebrows in Oxford and beyond.

The college is in North Oxford on the edge of the Parks, and its grounds, extending to the River Cherwell, are amongst the most beautiful in Oxford. It started with eight students, only a few books in the library and somewhat chaotic domestic arrangements. Now it has more than 400 students, and competition for entrance – merit is the only yardstick for admission – is very keen.

REGENT'S PARK COLLEGE

Behind its modest facade in Pusey Street, Regent's Park College has a fine range of buildings which well repay a visit. The college has the status of a Permanent Private Hall in the University, and is in membership with the Baptist Union of Great Britain.

It began in 1910 as Stepney Academy, but removed to Regent's Park in 1856 to be nearer the University of London – hence its name. In 1927, shortly before the expiration of the lease of its premises, the college moved to its present site in central Oxford, and it attained its present status in 1957. It exists primarily to train men for the Christian ministry, mainly of course in the Baptist churches at home and overseas, but it accepts students to read in disciplines other than theology. Its members take a full part, especially in sport, in the student life of Oxford. It is a meeting place for many professors and lecturers, especially from the USA, who through membership of the college, and through the University status of recognised student, have access to the libraries, lectures and life of the University during their sabbatical leave.

TEMPLETON COLLEGE

Templeton College was originally established as the Oxford Centre for Management Studies. It was renamed Templeton College in 1984 as a result of a benefaction from Mr John M. Templeton, a former Rhodes Scholar. The institution conducts research into management, undertakes executive development programmes for experienced senior executives and tutors University students for higher degrees in Management Studies and for the Honours degree in Engineering, Metallurgy, Economics and Management.

Originally incorporated in 1965 the college occupies a 37 acre site and its buildings contain not only residential accommodation but teaching rooms and a library which is open to all members of the University.

BOTANIC GARDEN

The college gardens form an incomparable setting for the historic buildings of Oxford. The University has its own garden near Magdalen Bridge, alongside the Cherwell, which is open to visitors and is in its own right a lovely and fascinating oasis in an area where traffic is heavy. But it has a remarkable history and is the oldest in Europe after Pisa and Leyden. It was founded by Lord Danby in 1621 on a three acre site as a centre for the growing of herbs used in medicine.

Since the middle of the 17th century it has been a centre for the cultivation of plants introduced from abroad, and is the place where the founders of the Royal Gardens at Kew and Rothamsted started their work. In one of the glasshouses, of which there are eight—all open to the public—the visitor can see such tropical plants as bananas being cultivated. In addition there are lovely rock and water gardens, and a historical collection of roses which shows the stages of their improvement to the magnificence of present-day blooms.

ST PETER'S COLLEGE

Founded as a Permanent Private Hall in 1929, the college reached the status of a fully independent college in 1961. When Convocation—then the chief legislative body of the University—agreed to this, it was the first time for 80 years that a new society had been admitted to the full privileges of a college. The history of the college goes back to the ministry at Oxford of the late Bishop Chavasse of Liverpool, first as Rector of St Peter-le-Bailey (the former parish church is now the college chapel), and then for the next ten years as Principal of Wycliffe Hall. One of the early benefactors was the late Lord Nuffield, who gave an undergraduate block in memory of his mother, Emily Morris. When the hall opened as a hostel for non-collegiate students, there were 13 of them. It has enjoyed the generosity of many notable supporters, and has extended greatly almost in the centre of the City of Oxford. It incorporates the old Canal House, once the headquarters of the former Canal Navigation Company. St Peter's makes a notable contribution to Oxford, as well as of graduates going into industry, finance and commerce. It has always had a high proportion of scientists among its fellows, and a high proportion of pupils from State schools is numbered among its membership.

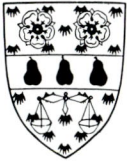

NUFFIELD COLLEGE

William Richard Morris, first Viscount Nuffield, creator of the vast motor-car organisation which then bore his name, had become by 1937 Oxford's greatest benefactor since the Middle Ages, and his gifts to the university and colleges could be counted in millions. He had often considered founding a college, and he had also roundly condemned the seedy approach to the centre of Oxford from the railway station, in particular the decaying wharf which was the terminal of the canal. When the opportunity offered in 1936, he bought the site and began negotiations with the university authorities about the foundation of a new college. His original idea was one devoted to engineering and the practical engineers, but there were difficulties which made such a scheme impracticable in Oxford, and he was told that the university would be greatly helped by the foundation of a college for post-graduates, devoted primarily to research in social studies, in which students could collaborate with practical men of affairs.

THE TOWN HALL   The present building, which was opened in May 1897 by King Edward VII, then Prince of Wales, stands on a site which has been occupied by the town's civic headquarters for 750 years.

OXFORD'S HISTORIC LANDMARKS

Martyrs Memorial and the church of St. Michael at the Northgate. Although the actual spot where Archbishop Cranmer, Bishop Ridley and Bishop Latimer were burnt at the stake in Queen Mary's reign is in Broad Street, marked by a stone cross in the roadway outside Balliol College, the chief monument to their memory was not raised until 1841. In that year the famous Martyrs' Memorial, a graceful cross in the style of those built by Edward I to commemorate his wife Queen Eleanor, was erected where St. Giles begins and in honour of the same event the north aisle of St. Mary Magdalene was also restored. Last century too, during excavations in Broad Street, the end of a wooden stake surrounded by ashes was found below the road where the cross is now inserted. It is exhibited in the Ashmolean Museum together with a massive hoop of iron believed to have been worn by Cranmer during his imprisonment. Another relic is to be found in the ancient church of St. Michael-at-the-Northgate, the door of the Archbishop's cell in Bocardo prison where he was confined. The Bocardo, demolished with the city's north gate in the eighteenth century, adjoined the church.

The ancient Church of St. Michael at the Northgate.

CARFAX TOWER

The tower, which dates from the reign of Edward III, is at the exact centre of ancient Oxford. It is all that is left on a site where stood a succesion of churches, the first of which was built in 1034. The tower is a favourite with tourists who, from the top, can get an unrivalled view of Oxford's skyline. Equally fascinating are the quarter-boys on the tower. They mark the passing of the hours, and were first mentioned in 1592. The originals are carefully preserved in the City and County Museum, their place on the tower having been taken by replicas.

THE MARTYRS' MEMORIAL

The nineteenth-century memorial to one of Oxford's outstanding historic events. It is a notable landmark in the city, a favourite meeting place for tourists—in its time the butt of many undergraduate pranks—and one of the most photographed subjects in Oxford.

COLLEGES and HALLS

UNIVERSITY
Its first endowment dates from 1249 when William of Durham bequeathed 310 marks to the university, the income from which was to maintain ten or more needy Masters of Arts studying Divinity.

BALLIOL
Founded by John Balliol of Barnard Castle and Dervorguilla his wife, parents of John Balliol, King of Scotland between 1263 and 1268.

MERTON
Founded in 1264 at Malden in Surrey for the support of its scholars at Oxford, by Walter de Merton, Bishop of Rochester and sometime Chancellor of England.

EXETER
Founded in 1314 by Walter de Stapledon, Bishop of Exeter.

ORIEL
Founded by Edward II on the suggestion of Adam de Brome, Clerk in the Chancery, in 1326.

QUEEN'S
Founded as a 'collegiate hall' in 1340 by Robert de Eglesfield, Chaplain to Philippa, wife of Edward III: he commended it to the patronage of the Queen 'and her successors for all time, the Queen Consorts of England'.

NEW COLLEGE
Founded in 1379 by William of Wykeham, Bishop of Winchester and sometime Chancellor of England.

LINCOLN
Founded in 1478 by Richard Fleming, Bishop of Lincoln, in 1427; reconstructed and re-endowed by Thomas Rotherham, Bishop of Lincoln, later Archbishop of York and Chancellor of England.

ALL SOULS
Founded by King Henry VI in 1438 with Henry Chichele, Archbishop of Canterbury, as co-founder.

MAGDALEN
Founded in 1458 by William of Waynflete, Bishop of Winchester and sometime Chancellor of England.

BRASENOSE
Founded in 1509 by William Smyth, Bishop of Lincoln, and Sir Richard Sutton of Prestbury in Cheshire.

CORPUS CHRISTI COLLEGE
Founded in 1517 by Richard Fox, Bishop of Winchester.

CHRIST CHURCH
Founded as Cardinal College by Cardinal Wolsey in 1525; refounded in 1532 as King Henry VIII's College; in 1546 united by the King with the new Cathedral, formerly at Osney, and established as 'Ecclesia Christi Cathedralis Oxon'.

TRINITY
Founded in 1554–5 by Sir Thomas Pope of Tittenhanger in Hertfordshire.

ST. JOHN'S
Founded in 1555 by Sir Thomas White, Alderman of the City of London.

ST PETER'S
Opened as a permanent private hall in 1929; became a full college in 1961 with its own Royal Charter of Incorporation.

WOLFSON
Established by University in 1965 for men and women graduates with benefactions from Wolfson and Ford foundations. Has special concern for promotion of studies in natural sciences.

ST ANTONY'S
Founded in 1948 as a graduate college specially concerned with studies relating to Western Europe, Latin America, Africa, Middle East and Far East. Granted Charter of Incorporation in 1953.

ST CROSS
Established in 1965 as a society in which men and women graduates read for advanced degrees and diplomas of the University.

LINACRE
Established in 1962 as Linacre House. Title changed to Linacre College in 1965. Its graduate students contain a high proportion from overseas.

MANCHESTER
Founded in Manchester in 1786 to provide higher education for dissenters. Came to Oxford in 1889; now a centre for mature students, granted the status of Permanent Private Hall in 1990.

JESUS
Founded by Queen Elizabeth by Letters Patent in 1571 on the petition of Dr. Hugh Price.

WADHAM
Founded by Nicholas Wadham of Mersfield, Somerset, and Dorothy his wife in 1612 under Letters Patent granted by King James I.

PEMBROKE COLLEGE
Founded in 1624 at the cost of charges of Thomas Tesdale of Glympton in Oxfordshire and Richard Wightwick, Rector of Ilsley, Berks.

WORCESTER
Founded under the will of Sir Thomas Cookes, Baronet, of Bentley Pauncefote, Worcestershire, in 1714.

HERTFORD
Originally Hart Hall founded about 1282; incorporated by Charter as Hertford College in 1740; became Magdalen Hall in 1805 and was refounded as Hertford College in 1874.

KEBLE
Founded in 1868 as a memorial to the Rev. John Keble, sometime Fellow and Tutor of Oriel College and Professor of Poetry at Oxford.

ST. EDMUND HALL
The last of the academical halls which first provided residence for scholars at Oxford: traditionally associated with St. Edmund of Abingdon, Archbishop of Canterbury, 1234–40. It was granted a Charter to become a college in 1957.

LADY MARGARET HALL
Founded in 1878 and opened the following year. Admitted a full college of the University in 1960.

SOMERVILLE
Founded in 1878 as Somerville Hall and admitted a full college in 1960.

ST. HUGH'S
Opened as St. Hugh's Hall in 1886 and admitted to full college status in 1959.

ST. HILDA'S
Founded as St. Hilda's Hall in 1893 and in 1960 admitted a full college of the University.

ST. ANNE'S
Founded as the Society of Oxford Home Students in 1879, becoming St. Anne's Society in 1942 and admitted to full college status in 1959.

ST. CATHERINE'S COLLEGE
Founded in 1868 for undergrauates who were not attached to any college or hall, becoming St. Catherine's Society in 1930. In 1963 it received a Charter of Incorporation as a college.

NUFFIELD COLLEGE
Founded by Lord Nuffield in 1937 as a college for post-graduate studies, receiving a Charter of Incorporation in 1958.

MANSFIELD
Founded in 1886 'to provide a Free Church faculty in theology at Oxford and a college for the training of dissenting Ministers'. Granted the status of a Permanent Private Hall in 1955.

GREEN
Opened in 1979 and built on site of Radcliffe Observatory in Woodstock Road. Foundation made possible by gift of nearly £2m from Dr Cecil H. Green. American industrialist and philanthropist and his wife.

CAMPION HALL
Permanent Private Hall for members of society of Jesus. Moved to present site in Brewer Street in 1935.

ST. BENET'S HALL
Foundation dates from 1897. Granted status of Permanent Private Hall in 1918. Governing Body is Abbot and Council of Ampleforth Abbey.

GREYFRIARS
A Franciscan Foundation, originally established in Oxford in 1224. Originally known as Grosseteste House.

REGENT'S PARK
Founded in 1810 as Baptist Academical Institution at Stepney. Moved to Regent's Park, London, in 1856 and assumed present title. Transferred to Oxford in 1927.

TEMPLETON COLLEGE
Founded in 1965 as The Oxford Centre for Management Studies to apply Oxford teaching methods and research to the disciplines of management. Name changed to Templeton College in 1984.

SHELDONIAN THEATRE

A unique glimpse of an outstanding occasion, the formal installation of the Rt Hon the Lord Jenkins of Hillhead as Chancellor, the chief officer of Oxford University, by the Vice-Chancellor, in the sumptuous setting of the Sheldonian Theatre.

In the semi-circle below sit the Heads of Houses, Doctors, and distinguished guests, while other leading university figures occupy seats in the area.

Undergraduates are prominent in the upper gallery.

THE COLLEGES and other buildings which comprise the university of Oxford, have become famous and places of pilgrimage for visitors from every corner of the globe, and to match the appeal of the architectural glories are the men and women who have studied within these ancient walls through the centuries.

Among them are many whose names are household words today.

Sir Walter Raleigh
Oriel College
(1552–1618)

The first Englishman who "led the way to a greater England beyond the seas"

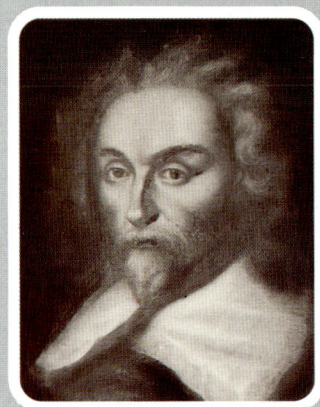

Dr William Harvey
Warden of Merton College (1645)

Discoverer of the circulation of the blood

John Radcliffe
University College
(1650–1714)

Leading physician of his day—left a fortune for charitable purposes. His name was immortalised at Oxford in the Radcliffe Camera, Radcliffe Infirmary and the Radcliffe Observatory

Sir Christopher Wren
Wadham College, later a Fellow of All Souls
(1632–1723)

One of the founders of the Royal Society. Chiefly remembered as the architect of London after the ravages of the great fire and most especially as architect of St Paul's Cathedral

John Wesley
(1703–1791)

Founder of the Methodist Church. Undergraduate at Christ Church. After being ordained he was elected a Fellow of Lincoln College where he began his life's work of evangelisation

Charles Dodgson
Christ Church
(1832–98)

Author and mathematician, best known for his immortal "Alice in Wonderland" stories written under pseudonym of Lewis Carroll

Sir Henry Maximilian Beerbohm
Merton College
(1890)

The inimitable "Max" author and cartoonist. His best remembered book is "Zuleika Dobson" with its Oxford setting

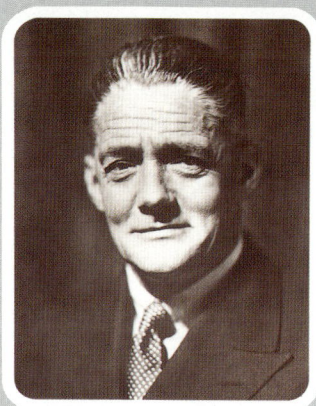

William Richard Morris
(1877–1963)

Created Lord Nuffield, founder of the motor car empire which bore his name. Began his career by repairing and making bicycles in a garden shed. The greatest benefactor the country has ever known—he gave away more than £25 million

Thomas Edward Lawrence
"Lawrence of Arabia" (1888–1935).
Jesus College

His knowledge of Arabia, where he had lived, enabled him to play a leading role in the war, recorded in his book "Seven Pillars of Wisdom"

Professor Edward Thomas Hall
CBE, FBA
Director of Research Laboratory for Archaeology & History of Art

His latest development was the Accelerator Mass Spectrometer for radio carbon dating which he used for dating the Turin Shroud

Margaret Thatcher
Somerville College

The first woman to become Prime Minister of Britain

Sir Roger Bannister

Became world-famous as the first man to run the mile in less than four minutes in 1954 on the University Running Track at Oxford

THE TWIN CITIES OF BONN, GERMANY AND OXFORD.
As a gift to commemorate the fortieth anniversary of the twinning of the university City with
Bonn, the capital of West Germany before the recent unification, Mr and Mrs Thomas presented
the Lord Mayor of Oxford, Mrs Betty Standingford with a giant enlargement of their famous
photograph of the city's "Golden Heart". The picture now hangs in Bonn Town Hall.